MEIN

DRUMPF

Crow Hollow Books

MEIN DRUMPF

Poems to Make America Great

JAY SIZEMORE

Published by Crow Hollow Books
Nashville, TN 37075

Copyright © 2016, Jay Sizemore

Manufactured print on demand

10 9 8 7 6 5 4 3 2 1

ISBN 978-1537687513

Cover design by Jay Sizemore.

Dedicated to the American Dream.

AMERICA THE QUIET

America, you're not so beautiful anymore.
Your mop water runs red,
bags under your eyes
so blue they're almost black,
but at least your skin is mostly white.
America, every day is your birthday.
Every meal is a birthday cake.
Your waist is shameless in its waste.
It's okay. You're lovable
even when you're unfuckable.

Did you hear the fireworks?
The neighbor's dog won't stop barking.
Ever wonder how many gunshots
go unnoticed in the noise,
how many bodies get found
days after the party subsides?
America, your breath reeks of beer,
and they named it after you.
It's okay. A car crash won't kill an idea.

America, I've stopped loving you,
even as you have stopped pretending to care
about anything other than yourself.
The fireworks flash in showers of spark
and awestruck mouths gasp in the glory
of their jellyfish embers, emblazoned
against a backdrop of indigo sky.
The charcoal briquets in the charcoal grills
turn gray and white with heat,
scents of seared meat and smoke
drift through the dew-drenched yards
of America, celebrating independence

from terror,
from suicide bombs,
from water scarcity,
from revolution.

America, I still believe in you,
even as sports stars and movie stars
and rock stars and rap stars
continue to let the homeless starve.
Even as we enslave ourselves
to the cell phone.
Even as rapists get lesser sentences
than simple possession charges.
America, can you hear the gunshots?
Can you hear the explosions?
The cries in other tongues?
There's a world apart from us,
and it is suffering.
America I need you.
I need to believe your silence
is indecision
and not indifference.

TABLE OF CONTENTS

AMERICA IS

a five hundred dollar vacuum cleaner.
a letter from a collection agency.
chemotherapy.

fireworks for the whole month of July.
a petition to save the drive-in.
short-term disability.

a single-serve coffee maker.
zero percent financing for the first six months.
glamorous infidelity.

breaking news.
a vaginal ultrasound.
a bubble blown to infinity.

LIVING HERE

is like watching Scarlett Johansson take an infinite shit
into Thomas Jefferson's dusty eye sockets.
It's the Great American Novel written on a matchbook
that will set the Constitution on fire.

Living here is living in a perpetual eating contest
where the only trophy is pride
and cancer is a rite of passage. It's a roulette wheel
of schools, with a bullet instead of a marble.

Black lungs and yellow water.
It's a church erected to Clint Eastwood and John Wayne
with pews of homosexual bones
and Native American peace pipes made into crosses.

All of my heroes are alcoholics or dead alcoholics.
All of my dreams are about sex.
All of my life is filling a casket with dollar bills.
All of the dollar bills will not pay for the funeral.

Living here is a Grand Canyon full of aluminum cans.
It's all Citizens United in song, a song only dogs can hear.

STRAWBERRY MOON

They couldn't wash the blood from the moon,
night of the summer solstice,
night of grim-set mouths, hands plunged deep
in silk-lined pockets, restless and rageless.

The camera phones lit faces in their windows
wanting to Instagram the memory
they wouldn't have tomorrow,
full moon dipped in transmission fluid,
globe luxation
of the god damned God.

Fifty-two senators *awe-shucks-ing*
their way to another list of names
fed through America's lotto machine
of human teeth and brass shell casings
rattling like death's labored lungs.

They'll show you pictures
of children lost so young,
their parents become living ghosts
of a slide projection reel,
haunting rooms of muted coughs
and anxious feet shuffling
to nowhere and for nothing.

Get your Lebron James jerseys,
before the next Powerball drawing,
before the heatwave
to end all heatwaves
burns down the redwoods
and every quiet place worth saving,
before the lightning bugs

sleep forever in the soil
rather than waste their light
on a world that doesn't want it.

This is the slow repetition of surrender
that pulls back the hammer
and places the gun to the temple
just because it can.

STAR-SPANGLED SINNER

~for C.K.

O, say can you see the bodies in the streets?
Red planets rising through draped white sheets.
Sold out stadiums still stand and applaud,
still hold hands over pride-swole hearts,
while the homeless hunt half-eat hotdogs
from dumpsters
and beg for change in parking lots.

Is this too preachy for you?
America the beautiful bowl of bloody piss?
America the drone strike bomber of the innocent?
America, where a busted tail light
is a cancer gone undiagnosed.
Where they watch hundreds drown
in capsized boats just off the Turkish coast
and do nothing except turn up their nose.
America, the Christ-like Nation of narcissists.

When were we ever great?
When we split the backs of the blacks we owned?
When we drove the Natives from their homes,
into cages, whiskey bottles and worthless fields?
When we were the first to drop the Bomb?
When we told women they couldn't decide
if part of themselves should live or die,
who could buy land, who could vote?
When we poisoned our own water supplies
and left the destitutes in their slums?

If you want me to stand and sing your song,
give me something to sing for!
The redwoods are burning, soon to be gone.

The tundras are thawing, soon to be gone.
A state of emergency is more than a flood.
America is dying.
Are you still in love?

GRAND CANYON CONVENIENCE

~after Walt Whitman

O canyon! Grand Canyon! the daylight slowly fades.
The final notes from a golden horn, ever so softly played.
Plans are drawn, crows are cawin', the curtain is falling
on a lifetime of erosion, a river's quiet calling.
It's death! Cold death!
The heart of a Coke machine!
To fill the land with quarters,
and give the cliffs gangrene.

O canyon! Grand Canyon! preserve your majesty,
in the face of destruction, one must lose their modesty.
They'd see your bosom marred with scarring,
a cancer of coffee beans and souvenir shop parking.
This canyon! Our canyon!
Is more than a Coke machine!
This land holds time's thread
traced through a river's vein.

The bulldozers idle growling dogs, iron teeth set on edge,
the canyon has no words but wind for its own defense.
They'll say that beauty, like memory, naturally fades,
they'll say this life is a sucker waiting to be played.
Stand up! Preserve majesty!
Defend beauty as if your spleen,
for when beauty is buried in change
we give our souls gangrene.

THE DAY NORTH KOREA BANNED POETRY

James Franco shed a tear, smearing the letter "q"
in his stern letter to Kim Jong Un.
Of course Franco writes his letters by hand,
by candle light if possible,
with a quill feather pen and ink well,
his fingers stained purple,
as if he has been eating plums.
He sends his letters by carrier pigeon.
Then he puts his penis in a paper sack
and writes "Not Fucking Any More"
on the bag with a sharpie.
Only men who have been raped
will get the joke. In his letter, James says,
"I once saved the world while high
and wearing a shirt that hadn't been washed
for at least seven days. I made Eddie Murphy
laugh, so your laws have no power over me."
North Korea banned laughter,
along with dioramas of dictators
dressed in drag. This put Russell Brand
out of business, so he started making t-shirts
asking for revolution. Franco tweeted his support,
which Seth Abramson re-tweeted,
and then someone wrote a think piece
on the significance of paperless billing.
Everything is connected because everything
is made of atoms that bond or don't bond
and at that level of existence James Bond
has his license to kill revoked.
My collection of atoms wants to bond
with your collection, and that means
I want to fuck you. Isn't that what life

is all about, until North Korea bans fucking,
and then James Franco stops writing
poems, which is what North Korea really wants
because metamodernism is a terrible joke
that people only pretend to get.

WHAT WAR IS GOOD FOR

War keeps the ground in business.
The leaves expect no adoration for dying,
they parachute down from the limbs
in slow, spiraling arcs of red and gold,
each death a signal flare in reverse.

War keeps sacrifice in style.
Like the leaves, kids leave home
and are blown in haphazard loops
toward different destinations
that end in the same place:
Khaki pants and fatigues.

War is a cure for boredom.
Flying drones in a video game:
Christians versus Muslims,
the American attempt
at making horror civilized
assaults my skin
until I'm desensitized,
awash in zeroes and ones.

War is the prayer that hangs
on my tongue
like a hair I can't find.
I see the torrents of blood
bled onto the desert rock,
the truckloads of people
driven and dumped
into the mass graves

and I think of the factory workers
responsible for each machine gun shell.

I think of the masked women
polishing the chrome warheads
to such a pristine shine.
I think of the manicured hands
that set the pin in each grenade.
War keeps food on America's plate,
just as it holds the curved blade to her throat
amid a forest of falling things
she once was convinced would grow back.

THOUGHTS AND PRAYERS

I prayed for a time machine,
to go back and replace sounds
of exploding gunpowder
with those of farts blown through silk,
every rifle shot now a raspberry,
a slobbery-lipped punchline
instead of a gorilla fist pounding.

I prayed that bullets might grow nerves,
that they might feel pain
and learn to deflect themselves
away from death,
like tiny Woody Allen's slumping
through crowded sidewalks
saying "excuse me" over and over.

I thought about changing,
but I asked you to instead,
I asked you to accept
the taste of blood in your drinking water.

I thought about numbers
and how meaningless they are
because numbers never learned to breathe.

I prayed for world peace,
for flocks of doves
to come fucking feather wing flapping
through Mitch McConnell's eyes,
white down raining like fake snow
in *It's a Wonderful Life*.

I prayed that Donald Trump

would admit he hates the color brown
with his tongue somewhere inside
Wayne LaPierre's mouth,
their hands lost in each other's pants,
working towards that climax
on their filigree fuck-bed
of the broken and the dead.

I thought about the law
and the end of the world,
and how symbiotic
flames flickered like daggers
in the veins of their bodies.

Mostly, I prayed for my wife
to buy me a Flesh Light,
to help America be great again,
the anarchic lubricant
of the nightly news,
another fake, warm hole
just wanting to be real
until even that dream is gone.

ODE TO JUSTICE ANTONIN SCALIA

(from his own mouth)

Words no longer have meaning,
nothing but interpretive jiggery-pokery
that makes flagpole sitting a fundamental right,
so get over it. Pure applesauce.

It's a pro-abortion novelty
to uphold Second Amendment rights,
deciding it's acceptable to execute the retarded,
the enduring Constitution of the adopted dead.

It's a reduction to the absurd
to not harbor moral feelings against homosexuality,
much like murder. I'm not a scientist.
To my critics, I say, "Vaffanculo."

Let 60,000 consenting adults
display their genitals to one another,
have them erect a conglomerate of the cross,
the star of David, and a Muslim half-moon.

Refuse jobs to haters of the Chicago Cubs,
to snail eaters and adulterers,
the gays don't have special rights.
It's fundamentally illogical to have gay sex.

States may permit abortion on demand. It's easy.
We can't cast a cloud on the legitimacy
of George Bush's election.
I would hide my head in a bag.

This Supreme Court has descended
to the mystical aphorisms of the fortune cookie.

It's attributable to racial entitlement.
Jesus Christ believed in the Devil. Case closed.

THE ILLUSION OF STARTING OVER

The new leaf is the same as the old leaf,
though each life feels variant and unique.
Just flipping a page on the calendar,
and writing the wrong date on the check,

popping a cork on a bottle of cheap champagne,
white suds spilling down the green glass neck,
we sing of old acquaintances, long forgot,
and raise a glass for another day of the week.

Time itself is devoid of chance,
that infinite wheel of infinite spokes spinning
never stops and never slows,
never resets to zero, because midnight is a myth.

Throw away your watch, smash all the clocks,
break every bone in your fist against the gallows,
for when it comes to changing your mind,
today is the same as it will be tomorrow.

THE BLOODIED BOY AND THE GAMES

Can you hit the water like a knife,
so sharp and so quiet
it remains oblivious to the stabbing?
     No somersaults by choice.
     Every building a potential grave,
     a rubble of tombstones disarrayed.

Can you run faster than death,
with a nation of gasps
riding your shoulders and spine?
     Here, a gold medal for a sunrise.
     We wipe the blood from our eyes.
     We dig our children free of debris
     and carry them like bombs.

Are you sure you picked the right God?
Has the arrow loosed itself
from behind your ear
and found the center of the universe?
Doesn't the ocean sound like applause?
     There are so many that are lost.
     Their names vanish like landscape details
     pulled further and further away.
     This fog makes blind strangers of us all
     bruised bodies hurting to be touched.

Is the world watching?
I've balanced my entire life
upon a beam no wider
than the average human foot.
I've turned myself into a compass,
a needle floating inside a leaf.

17

I've conditioned my frame,
hardened my senses
through repetition,
becoming an instrument
of precision
lifting fighter jets
up over my head.
Will you fold my indiscretions into a flag,
while a black man bites the curb,
and forgive me for being great?
       Stare into his eyes.
       Dark as polished stone,
       the blank gaze
       of a shell-shocked child,
       his blood dried to his cheek
       like an unwanted birthmark
       not given at birth.
       It's no mistake that the human heart
       is larger than a grenade.
       Are you sure you picked the right God?

ANONYMOUS LETTER TO DONALD TRUMP FROM THE FBI:

"You better take it, before your filthy,
abnormal fraudulent self is bared
to the nation." -from an 'anonymous'
letter written to Martin Luther King

TRUMP:

Your behavior is low-grade, abnormal,
ill-deserved of admiration or respect,
I shall not dignify your name
with common courtesy,
you call to mind the trumpets of doom,
golden horns sounding
and tearing holes in the sky.

Your heart is a fraud,
your ribs are made of glass,
your life is a liability to hope.
No God would create you.

You would like to have the throne,
to call yourself a leader,
but you are dissolute, immoral, an imbecile.
Obama made America great.
You built casinos and hotels
with your father's money.
You are bankrupt. You are done.

Put your psychotic ear to the enclosure,
listen to history being written without you.
Your memory is already fading,
ex-wives spreading legs for pyramids,

abnormal interests in daughters,
you are an animal, devoid of humanity,
you are finished, you are done.

It's all on the record,
your church of filth,
your beastly devolution.
Time will prove you irrelevant, phony, a joke.
There's one way out of this,
one way to escape the swirling drain.
Withdraw, admit your mistake.

NEVER FORGET

the slurpee machine and its soothing hum,
a lullaby of monotonous machination,
belts and fans turning endlessly
to crush the ice, to churn the syrup.

Never forget the buzzing neon of the OPEN sign,
the on and off glow of COLD BEER
flickering in the window like a lighthouse strobe,
calling the sneakered cattle through the doors

at all hours, their footsteps squeaking,
an erratic metronome working
against the polished reflective tile,
as ceaseless as shovels in a graveyard.

Never forget the potato chip vendors,
their rolling racks of plastic-bagged crunch,
preservatives and salt, sugars and starch,
keeping the shelves stocked with tasty death.

Never forget the Indians, the Pakistanis,
the pimple-faced teenagers who sacrifice
selflessly, countless nights and weekends
to the dream of, "Thank you, come again."

Never forget parking lots, wet concrete and gasoline fumes,
oil stains between white painted lines,
while inside it's hot dogs on heated conveyors
and mop water splashed with bleach,

the clickety ticker tape noise
of lottery tickets dispensed from a dial,

and the ringing bells of the change drawers
singing the music of the American anthem.

TO RUSSIA WITH LOVE

Russia, I've lost my car keys,
Russia, I've lost my cat.
Help me retrace my steps,
across that blue
Slushpuppy sea,
brain freeze!

Across frozen tundra
where every footfall
is a box of broken light bulbs
crushed by your weight,
the North Star
can be your selfie stick
leading you off the cliff
of boring self-righteousness.

Oh, President Putin!
If you find my cat,
put him in your lap.
Stroke his skull
against those washboard abs.
My cat is homosexual
and will enjoy your horse scent
affinity for shirtlessness.

Russia, have you shaved your pits?
Has your shrubbery been maintained?
I've lost my will to live
on this continent,
while most continue to devolve
into chaos deserts,
post-apocalyptic
fictions turned prophecies

happening even as they're denied.

There's a wildfire in my eyes,
I swear I'm not crying.
Russia, I've lost my mind,
is that treason?
Is it treason to love America
more than my mother?
To ejaculate red, white, and blue?
Russia, take my hand,
I've lost the narrative thread,
and you could be the needle
pushed through the flesh
that conjoins these eyelids.

Russia, there you are.
Just where I left you,
the last place I would ever
think to look.

THE BODY AS AN OBJECT OF DESIRE

~for Melania Trump

Erections are hard to hide
in flat front pants,
this body a betrayal,
a self-inflicted wound
that arouses sharp senses
like stigmata for sex.

This is what I want.
To be wanted,
to see myself reflected
in stainless steel,
in eyes overcome with lust
like a sensory cataract,
to feel worshiped
just for inhabiting
physical space.

Are you human, or are you dancer?
Are you animal, or are you violence?
Everyone's a mess of brush strokes
slapped mad dash
across years of canvas
rolled from a spool
that may or may not
run out before this line is read.

What purpose does shame serve?
The body gets what it wants
one way or another.
When it stops
the stars reclaim
what was always theirs.

So speak your truth,
seek your truth,
shed your garments in a crowd.
Fuck and be fucked,
feel more alive for the fucking.
The sun belongs to no one.
The moon lives in our moans.
Some day we'll look back
and wish we had felt more.

ANTON CHIGURH DECIDES THE FATE OF THE ELECTION

~after Cormac McCarthy

Friendo, this quarter was stamped with a date
the day it was made. Since then, it has traveled.
Who knows how many hands, how many pockets,
how many lives, carried it, or were carried.
What it bought over time.

People think I am the angel of Death.
But I'm just the messenger.
How much would you pay
for a glass of water?
The sky leeches it from you.
Hang your tongue out the window like a dog.
Wash your hands in poison,
they'll never be clean.
Something seems obvious about that.

What's the most you ever lost in a coin toss?
Your whole life summed up
in a quick flick of the wrist.
Do you feel that hair bristling
at the back of your neck?
That's recognition. Staring into the eyes
of a wolf, knowing the campfire is burning out,
knowing that the wolf is just a man
draped in fur and desperation, thirst and hunger.

Every day is a bet against time,
a bet you will lose, so risk everything.
Tell the murderers to fuck themselves.
Call out the liars.

Let the wolves drink rain water
from your hands.
From the tap, it tastes like gasoline.
You've been on a winning streak
every morning you've opened your eyes.

There's a darkness that waits
like a world without breath.
The entire future of existence
drawn into the head of a match,
and someday, someone will strike it,
fearing blindness, that suffocating caul.

These rules are yokes
chaining us to the weight we carry.
That's the sound of everything
you've ever done, dragged
like a dead Cadillac behind you,
such a long, rutted road
of triumph, of loss, the universe.

This coin is a symbol of fate.
Such a slender representation of choice,
either/or
resting between my thumb and forefinger,
cold, objective and plain,
primed for release by powers
greater than those dirty hands
segregating the lucky
from the unlucky.
Do you know what is at stake?
Everything or nothing.
So, call it.

THE FIRST

~for HRC

The first woman could talk to snakes,
she accepted their gifts
and made love to knives.

The first woman cut a hole
in the ceiling that wasn't there
with a diamond large as hope.

She pulled herself up
by her bootstraps
and stood on the other side

of the sky, filled with balloons
and music and little girls' eyes
swollen with tearful pride

at the thought of selling out
to an idea, becoming
nothing but a box to check,

a hero in a white pant suit
stalling the moon
with promises of an endless night,

and her fingers crossed
for more time
to win the love of the undecided.

DONALD TRUMP HAS A DREAM:
A PRESIDENTIAL INAUGURATION
SPEECH
~ after MLK

My fellow Americans, I am happy to join you today
in celebrating the second greatest moment
in human history:
the day you elect me as President of these United States,
second only to the day of my birth, the day God smiled
his brightest smile, brighter than the Big Bang
which of course never happened.

Some years ago, six to be exact, the Supreme Court,
which casts its great shadow over every vagina,
overturned Citizens United. This decree was *HUGE,*
granting every corporation a birth certificate,
finally freeing billionaires
to buy politicians like shares of penny stocks.

But even now billionaires must struggle in secret
for the joys of owning a country.
Even now there are those blocking traffic,
holding up cardboard signs,
shouting "Black Lives Matter."
Even now 99 percent of this nation
feels entitled to their fair share of the ocean,
the wealth we sweat out of the slaves.
Hey, don't blame us because we're better than you.

Some people think the White House is a bank,
writing blank checks
on the backs of the Constitution
and the Declaration of Independence.
Hey, get a job.

The Hand-Out Bank for Freeloaders is bankrupt,
corrupt, all those checks are about to bounce.
If you're gonna put your name on something,
put it on greatness,
an idea you wear like a shark skin suit.
Failure is just another mortar
between the bricks of the walls
we'll build around Texas.

This is not the time to condemn the KKK.
This is not the time to accept Muslim prayer.
This is not the time to get hair plugs.
We must raise ourselves out of the quicksand
of socialism and onto the Plymouth rock
of the Founding Fathers' erections.

If the blacks and the Mexicans
want to riot and rape
let them do it
in the ghettos they were born in.
America deserves to be great,
embossed in gold,
spray tanned.
America is a casino that always wins.

At the same time, I love everybody.
The blacks love me.
I love Mexican food.
If you want to stab a colored girl,
at least drag her out of the room first.
I don't want to see that.

We must not hate all Muslims
for causing 9/11.
We just have to kill the terrorists

and then kill their families
and their families' families.
That's how you end terrorism.
Every American must pledge
to buy a gun and sleep
with it under their pillow.

People ask me, "When will you be satisfied?"
And I tell them, "That's easy.
Soon as this country is great again.
Soon as the dollar is worth more
than the Euro. Soon as China
calls me up and begs *ME* for a loan.
Soon as Russia puts America
back on speed dial."

I know times are tough,
and just getting tougher.
But hard work is itself
a form of redemption.
Go home tonight and lose yourself
in the task at hand,
the task of building something
bigger than yourself,
the Great Pyramid of Trump.

Even though the future is uncertain
as a Magic 8 ball filled with tomorrows,
I believe in the American Dream.
My dream is your dream is your dream.

I have a dream that this nation will find God,
that the Bible can replace every school book,
that science and math become Sunday Studies,
that people realize Global Warming is a scam.

I have a dream that in the deserts of Nevada
casino owners and congressmen
can both be served by drunk Indians
at the buffet tables of fortune,
that the Small Pox blankets of the past
can become the fur rugs of the future.

I have a dream that my billionaire friends
can be judged not by the size of their towers,
not by the shades of their spray tans,
not by the thickness of their comb-overs,
but by the content of their wallets.
That my children can travel to Africa
to kill the elephants, the lions, the black rhinos,
and display their trophies with pride
in the sunsets of the Serengeti.

This is a good dream. Best you ever heard.

I have a dream that one day on Twitter,
a billionaire can share posts
of white supremacists
without being hassled by leagues
of black kids thinking they owe them an apology.

This is a good dream. Best you ever heard.

I have a dream that every hill and every valley,
every creek and every river,
every house and every street
will carry the emblem of my name,
trademarked for glory
like The Beatles dipped in glitter,
or a whore set on fire.

This is the hope of America.

Not the hope of Obama,
who said the Confederate Flag has got to go.

Remember that classic song,
when people loved the radio:
   Your loving give me a thrill,
   but loving don't pay my bills.

Every American knows the truth.

So let it rain from the Trump Tower of Chicago.
Let it rain from the Trump Tower of Vegas.
Let it rain from the Trump Towers of New York.
Let it rain from the Trump Towers yet to be built.

When it stops raining, we'll just make more,
this country is our dancer
shaking its ass for more,
so make it rain from the Trump Tower
replacing the White House.
Make it rain from the Trump Tower
once known as Capitol Hill.
Make it rain from the Trump Tower
of the Pentagon
and what was once the Supreme Court.

When we hear that bell tolling all across the land,
everyone will stand and sing:
   The best things in life are free,
   but you can keep em for the birds and bees.

ACKNOWLEDGEMENTS

Poems in this work originally appeared in the following publications: "America is," *Electric Windmill*; "Living here" and "The day North Korea banned poetry," *Black Heart Magazine*; "Strawberry moon," "Grand Canyon convenience," *Scarlet Leaf Review*; "Ode to Justice Antonin Scalia," "The bloodied boy and the games," *New Verse News*; "What war is good for," *TruthDig*; "The illusion of starting over," *Indiana Voice Journal*; "Anton Chigurh decides the fate of the election," *Wilderness House Literary Review.*

ABOUT THE AUTHOR

Jay Sizemore was born blue, raised by wolves, and learned to write by translating howls. He doesn't regret his wisdom teeth. He thanks you for your concern. His work can be found here or there, mostly there. Find him at jaysizemore.com, or, if you're a stalker, in Nashville, TN, where he may or may not really exist.